The
of love

Life minus love equals zero.
George Sweeting

If you want your life to
amount to something,
make sure love is part of
the equation.

Love is a powerful force

*Flood waters can't drown love,
torrents of rain can't
put it out.*
Song of Solomon 8:7, MGE

*Love does not die easily. It
is a living thing. It thrives
in the face of all of life's
hazards, save one – neglect.*
James D. Bryden

True love is
a constant

Love is not love
Which alters when it alteration finds,
Or bends with the remover to remove.
O, no! It is an ever-fixed mark,
That looks on tempests and is never
shaken.

I love thee, I love but thee; with a love
that shall not die; till the sun grows
cold and the stars grow old.
William Shakespeare

Love is selfless

Love is when the other person's happiness is more important than your own.
H. Jackson Brown Jr

God first, others second, self last.

Love gives and doesn't count the cost

Love seeketh not itself to please,
Nor for itself hath any care,
But for another gives it ease,
And builds a Heaven in Hell's despair.
William Blake

You can give without loving, but you cannot love without giving.

Love is like a loaf of bread?

Love doesn't just sit there like a stone; it has to be made, like bread, remade all the time, made new.
Ursula K. LeGuin

So keep kneading!

Love forgives

*Love is not blind, it sees
   more not less;
But because it sees more it
   chooses to see less.*
Anon

Focus on the roses
and not the thorns.

The desire to be loved is a powerful instinct

If there is anything better than to be loved, it is loving.
Anon

But remember, it is more blessed to give than to receive.

To ensure success in marriage . . .

God, the best maker of all
*   marriages,*
Combine your hearts into one.
William Shakespeare

Make sure God is a member of the partnership.

In marriage, one plus one equals one

For what thou art is mine;
Our state cannot be sever'd; we are one,
One flesh; to lose thee were to lose
*   myself.*
John Milton

So they are no longer two, but
one. Therefore what God has joined
together, let man not separate.
(Matthew 19:6.)

No holds barred

One half of me is yours,
the other half yours –
Mine own, I would say;
but if mine, then yours,
And so all yours!
William Shakespeare

Marriage means
100% commitment
to your partner.

All things being equal . . .

Marriage is that relation between man and woman in which the independence is equal, the dependence mutual, and the obligation reciprocal.
Louis K. Anspacher

Make sure there's plenty of give and take.

Adam's rib

Eve was not taken out of Adam's head to top him, neither out of his feet to be trampled on by him, but out of his side to be equal with him, under his arm to be protected by him, and near his heart to be loved by him.
Matthew Henry

Marriage is a union of two equal partners.

With God's help . . .

*Be the mate God
designed you to be.*
Anthony T. Evans

Be the best wife
you can be.

Be reasonable!

*A perfect wife is one
who doesn't expect a
perfect husband.*
Anon

You're not perfect, so you
shouldn't expect perfection in
others – even your husband!

Forgiveness is important

A good marriage is the union of two forgivers.
Ruth Graham

Make forgiveness part of your daily routine.

Forgive . . .

Once a woman has forgiven
a man, she must not reheat
his sins for breakfast.
Marlene Dietrich

And FORGET!

If you've caused hurt . . .

Next to the wound,
what women make best
is the bandage.
Jules Barbey d'Aurevilly

Make sure you start the
healing process.

It's good to talk . . . but sometimes it's better to keep quiet

To keep your marriage brimming,
With love in the loving cup,
Whenever you're wrong admit it;
Whenever you're right shut up.
Ogden Nash

Make sure you learn to tell the right time!

The recipe for a perfect wife . . .

Be trustworthy

Her husband has full confidence in her . . . She brings him good, not harm, all the days of her life.
Proverbs 31:11, 12

Be an influence for good and not evil.

Be industrious . . .

*She . . . works with
eager hands.*
Proverbs 31:13

. . . and approach hard work
with enthusiasm.

A woman's work is never done . . .

She gets up while it is still dark; she provides food for her family . . .
Proverbs 31:15

And sometimes she has to do a nightshift!

Be a good money manager

She considers a field and buys it; out of her earnings she plants a vineyard.
Proverbs 31:16

Use your financial resources wisely.

Keep working!

She sets about her work vigorously; her arms are strong for her tasks.
Proverbs 31:17

Energetic work pays dividends.

Don't forget to be charitable

*She opens her arms to
the poor and extends
her hands to the needy.*
Proverbs 31:20

Be hospitable and generous
to everyone.

Weigh your words before you speak

She speaks with wisdom, and faithful instruction is on her tongue.
Proverbs 31:26

Let your words be a source of blessing to others.

Get your priorities right

Charm is deceptive, and beauty is fleeting; but a woman who fears the LORD is to be praised.
Proverbs 31:30

Worry more about what's happening inside than what appears on the outside.

Always do your best . . .

Be to her virtues very kind,
Be to her faults a little blind.
Matthew Prior

But remind your husband
(and yourself) from time to
time that you're only human!

To ensure your husband stays at home . . .

Better to live on a corner of the roof than share a house with a quarrelsome wife.
Proverbs 21:9

Make sure you don't turn into a nag.

Your most vital role

The hand that rocks the cradle is the hand that rules the world.
W. R. Wallace

The importance of motherhood can't be overstated.

Motherhood makes women beautiful

My mother was the most beautiful woman I ever saw. All I am I owe to my mother. I attribute all my success in life to the moral, intellectual and physical education I received from her.
George Washington

This is the kind of beauty to strive for – one that won't fade with the passing years.

Motherhood
is costly

*Making the decision to have
a child – it's momentous. It
is to decide forever to have your
heart go walking outside your body.*
Elizabeth James

With children there will be
heartache as well as joy.

Motherhood means self-sacrifice

A mother is a person who, seeing there are only four pieces of pie for five people, promptly announces she never did care for pie.
Tenneva Jordan

You'll give, and joy in giving, never counting the cost.

You are being watched!

Children have never been very good at listening to their elders, but they have never failed to imitate them.
James Baldwin

Make sure you're a role model worth copying!

Instruction is important

Train a child in the way he should go, and when he is old he will not turn from it.
Proverbs 22:6

Early lessons are not soon forgotten.

Avoid constant criticism

*Children need models
more than they need critics.*
Joseph Joubert

Set a good example and
always give words of
encouragement.

Who ever said parenthood was easy?

Before I got married I had six theories about bringing up children; now I have six children and no theories.
John Wilmot, Earl of Rochester

Parenthood might be the biggest challenge of your life, but don't despair, as you have a Father of your own who promises to help you.

No advance instruction courses available!

Having children makes you no more a parent than having a piano makes you a pianist.
Michael Levine

Make sure you ask continual help from your Guide.

Make prayer a priority

Did mothers but realise the importance of their mission, they would be much in secret prayer, presenting their children to Jesus, imploring his blessing upon them, and pleading for wisdom to discharge aright their sacred duties.
E. G. White

Remember: *The prayer of a person living right with God is something powerful to be reckoned with.*
(James 5:16, MGE.)

Pray without ceasing

I remember my mother's prayers and they have always followed me. They have clung to me all my life.
Abraham Lincoln

The power and influence of prayer cannot be measured.

Mothers inspire men
to do great things . . .

*All that I am or ever hope to
be, I owe to my angel Mother.*
Abraham Lincoln

Aim, with the help of the
Lord, to be an inspiration to
your children.

Handle with care!

Bitter are the tears of a child:
Sweeten them. Deep are the thoughts
of a child: Quiet them. Sharp is the
grief of a child: Take it from him.
Soft is the heart of a child: Do
not harden it.
Pamela Glenconner

God has given you a precious
treasure. Be careful how you
nurture it.

A precious charge

*Children are the heritage of the Lord,
and we are answerable to him for
our management of his property.
The education and training of their
children to be Christians is the
highest service that parents can
render to God. It is a work that
demands patient labour – a lifelong,
diligent and persevering effort.*
E. G. White

Remember, your children belong firstly
to God and secondarily to you.

A mother's love

Before you were conceived
  I wanted you
Before you were born I loved you.
Before you were here an hour I
  would die for you.
This is the miracle of life.
Maureen Hawkins

A love so absolute, it mirrors the
love God has for his children – after
all, he *did* die for you.

How important are women?

Women are the real architects of society.
Harriet Beecher Stowe

If this is true, make sure you follow the Master Architect's blueprints.

Are you well organised?

I hate women because they always know where things are.
Voltaire

Where would the men be without us?

There's no place like home

Out of the dreariness,
Into its cheeriness,
Come we in weariness,
Home.
Stephen Chalmers

Make sure yours is a warm
and welcoming place.

Home is where the heart is

A house is made of walls and beams; a home is built with love and dreams.
Anon

Make sure yours is a place governed by love.

A woman's work is never done!

Work is either fun or drudgery. It depends on your attitude. I like fun.
Colleen C. Barrett

Adopt a positive attitude and the work won't seem so bad!

The work
has to be done

*Housekeeping is like being
caught in a revolving door.*
Marcelene Cox

But try not to go
round in circles!

A thankless task?

Housework is something you do that nobody notices until you don't do it.
Anon

Nevertheless . . . *Whatever you do, do well.* (Ecclesiastes 9:10, NLT.) There's always satisfaction in a job well done.

See God even in the little things

Teach me, my God and King,
in all things thee to see,
and what I do in anything
to do it as for thee.
George Herbert

Remember, *whatever you do,*
do it all for the glory of God
(1 Corinthians 10:31).

Always do your best

Whatever your task is, put your whole heart and soul into it, as into work done for the Lord and not merely for men – knowing that our real reward will come from him.
Colossians 3:23, 24, JBP

Half-hearted effort will bring half-baked results.

Put your back into it!

O Lord, you give us
everything at the
price of an effort.
Leonardo da Vinci

The Lord will provide . . .
but he expects us to play
our part as well.

Learn a lesson from the birds

God gives every bird its food,
but he does not throw it into
its nest.
J. G. Holland

Yes, trust God to provide for you,
but you have to take the first step.
Anything achieved without effort
is not really valued.

Weary of all the chores?

I am thankful for a lawn that needs mowing, windows that need cleaning and gutters that need fixing because it means I have a home. . . . I am thankful for the piles of laundry and ironing because it means my loved ones are nearby.
Nancie J. Carmody

Be grateful for what you have!

We all need to feel valued

The deepest craving of human nature is the need to be appreciated.
William James

And remember, *you* are precious in God's sight and the very hairs of your head are numbered (Matthew 10:30).

Three
things . . .

*Three things in human life are
important. The first is to be kind.
The second is to be kind. The third
is to be kind.*
Henry James

Let the kindness principle govern
all your actions.

Never a waste of time

Love and kindness are never wasted. They always make a difference. They bless the one who receives them, and they bless you, the giver.
Barbara de Angelis

Give and receive the blessings!

Guilty or
not guilty?

*If you were arrested for being
kind, would there be enough
evidence to convict you?*
Anon

Make sure you're guilty as
charged!

As you sow . . .

*The person who sows
seeds of kindness enjoys
a perpetual harvest.*
Anon

. . . so you reap.

The boomerang effect?

Those who bring sunshine into the lives of others, cannot keep it from themselves.
J. M. Barrie

What you give out
you will receive back.

Measure
for measure

Give, and it will be given to you.
good measure, pressed down, shaken
together and running over, will be
poured into your lap. For with the
measure you use, it will be measured
to you.
Luke 6:38

Giving is wise economy.

The sweet smell of generosity?

The fragrance always stays in the hand that gives the rose.
Hada Bejar

Generosity is as much a blessing to the giver as to the one who receives.

Freely you have received . . .

We must not only give what we have; we must also give what we are.
Désiré Joseph Mercier

Don't stint in giving of yourself to others.

Never,
never, never!

Have a heart that never hardens,
and a temper that never tires, and
a touch that never hurts.
Charles Dickens

Kindness, gentleness, patience
– cultivate these fruits of the
Spirit.

Wish you were beautiful?

God's fingers can touch nothing but to mould it into loveliness.
George MacDonald

Let God's Spirit work in you and you will be.

Want to hang on to your looks?

Cheerfulness and content are great beautifiers, and are famous preservers of good looks.
Charles Dickens

Being kind and cheerful may well help to halt the ageing process a little.

True beauty

Don't be concerned about the outward beauty of fancy hairstyles, expensive jewelry, or beautiful clothes. You should clothe yourselves instead with the beauty that comes from within, the unfading beauty of a gentle and quiet spirit, which is so precious to God.
1 Peter 3:3, 4, NLT

This kind of beauty won't fade.

Fancy some new clothes?

Therefore, as God's chosen people, holy and dearly loved, clothe yourselves with compassion, kindness, humility, gentleness and patience.
Colossians 3:12

Clothe yourself with God's designer wear.

Inner beauty

People are like stained-glass windows. They sparkle and shine when the sun is out, but when the darkness sets in, their true beauty is revealed only if there is a light from within.
Elizabeth Kübler-Ross

Let Jesus, the Light of the world, dwell in you and shine out from you.

Prioritise!

*I tell you, do not worry about your
life, what you will eat or drink; or
about your body, what you will wear.
. . . But seek first his kingdom and his
righteousness, and all these things
will be given to you as well.*
Matthew 6:25, 33

Put God first and don't worry
about *anything*.

Don't worry – it may never happen!

When I look back on all these worries, I remember the story of the old man who said on his deathbed that he had had a lot of trouble in his life, most of which had never happened.
Winston Churchill

Never trouble trouble till trouble troubles you!

Worry is useless!

Worry is like a rocking chair
– it gives you something to
do but it doesn't get you
anywhere.
Glenn Turner

Stop worrying and devote your
time to something that'll get
you somewhere!

Worry is like photography?

Worry is the darkroom in which negatives are developed.
Anon

For positive development, get out into the sunlight of his presence.

It's an ill wind . . .

Don't tell me that worry doesn't do any good. I know better. The things I worry about don't happen.
Anon

But remember, if you *don't* worry, it still won't happen!

If you worry you do not trust . . .

I believe God is managing affairs and that he doesn't need any advice from me. With God in charge, I believe everything will work out for the best in the end. So what is there to worry about?

Henry Ford

If you trust you do not worry.

Look back
and remember

*Let gratitude for the past
inspire us with trust for
the future.*
François Fénelon

Look ahead and trust!

How to cope with difficulties?

Tackle life's problems by trusting God's promises.
Anon

Are you standing on the promises?

Are you a champion worrier?

If worrying were an Olympic sport, you'd get the gold for sure.
Stephenie Geist

Devote your energies to something much more productive. Keep spiritually fit by trusting in God.

Stop worrying

You can throw the whole weight of your anxieties upon him, for you are his personal concern.
1 Peter 5:7, JBP

Let go and let God.

Prayer is the answer, no matter what the question

Keep looking up, for he is always looking down.
Anon

Make sure you stay in contact with God to get the answer.

Worried about the future?

*Do not be afraid of tomorrow,
for God is already there.*
Anon

Maybe you don't know what
tomorrow holds, but you know
who holds tomorrow.

Worried about the past?

You can't change the past but you can ruin the present by worrying about the future.
Anon

What's done is done. Focus on today and tomorrow which you *can* change.

Worried about today?

We can easily manage if we will only take, each day, the burden appointed to it. But the load will be too heavy for us if we carry yesterday's burden over again today, and then add the burden of the morrow before we are required to bear it.
John Newton

Remember that Jesus said, *'Sufficient unto the day . . .'*
Worry never robs tomorrow of its sorrow, it only saps today of its joy.
Leo F. Bascaglia

The secret of longevity?

If you ask what is the single most important key to longevity, I would have to say it is avoiding worry, stress and tension. And if you didn't ask me, I'd still have to say it.
George Burns

Worrying is bad for your health.

Forget your own troubles

The best cure for worry, depression, melancholy, brooding, is to go deliberately forth and try to lift with one's sympathy the gloom of somebody else.
Arnold Bennett

When you look at others' troubles, your own don't seem so momentous.

At the end of your tether?

I can do all things through Christ who strengthens me.
Philippians 4:13, NKJV

Claim that promise and
you can do it!
Remember, *Man's extremity
is God's opportunity.*
John Flavel

Why worry when you can pray?

Pray, and let God worry.
Martin Luther

When life gets too hard to
stand . . . *kneel.*

All talk and no prayer?

Have you prayed about your problem as much as you have talked about it?
Anon

Prayer is not a last extremity, it's a first necessity.

Shape your worries into prayers

Don't fret or worry. Instead of worrying, pray. Let petitions and praises shape your worries into prayers, letting God know your concerns. Before you know it, a sense of God's wholeness, everything coming together for good, will come and settle you down. It's wonderful what happens when Christ displaces worry at the centre of your life.
Philippians 4:6, 7, MGE

Put Christ first and he'll sort out your problems.

Make sure you have things in perspective

Any concern too small to be turned into a prayer is too small to be made into a burden.
Corrie ten Boom

Worry often gives small things a big shadow. Get out of the shadow into the sunlight.

Don't make a mountain out of a molehill

It's a good idea not to major in minor things.
Anthony Robbins

You'll find life's journey much easier if you don't have to go mountaineering every day.

The secret of the worry-free life?

Blessed is the person who is too busy to worry in the daytime and too sleepy to worry at night.
Anon

Keep busy, get your sleep, and stay connected to the One who can fix your problems.

The cure
for worry?

Worry is spiritual short sight.
Its cure is intelligent faith.
Paul Brunton

Be wise. Believe and trust
and be long-sighted!

Get yourself connected!

I keep the telephone of my mind open to peace, harmony, health, love and abundance. Then, whenever doubt, anxiety or fear try to call me, they keep getting a busy signal – and soon they'll forget my number.
Edith Armstrong

Make sure you give worry the engaged signal.

Cultivate a
cheerful disposition

The greater part of our happiness or
misery depends on our dispositions
and not our circumstances.
Martha Washington

Follow Paul's example – *I've learned*
by now to be quite content whatever
my circumstances. I'm just as happy
with little as with much, with much
as with little.
(Philippians 4:12, MGE.)

Accentuate
the positive . . .

*We spend precious hours fearing
the inevitable. It would be wise
to use that time adoring our
families, cherishing our friends,
and living our lives.*
Maya Angelou

And eliminate the negative!

A trade in?

Christ is not only a remedy for your weariness and trouble, but he will give you an abundance of the contrary, joy and delight.
Jonathan Edwards

Trade in the world's troubles for God's peace and joy.

Forget your troubles

*What a world this would
be if we could forget our
troubles as easily as we
forget our blessings.*
Anon

But remember and be grateful
for your blessings every day.

Are you good at arithmetic?

The hardest arithmetic to master is that which enables us to count our blessings.
Eric Hoffer

Make sure you learn to add up.

Need sailing lessons?

I'm not afraid of storms, for I'm learning to sail my ship.
Louisa May Alcott

Make sure you have the right Captain at the helm.

The serendipity effect

If you ever find happiness by hunting for it, you will find it, as the old woman did her best spectacles, safe on her own nose all the time.
Josh Billings

We miss out on so much happiness because we're looking for it in the wrong places.

The secret to having it all?

To have more, desire less.
Martin Luther

Focus your eyes on Heaven and the things of this world won't seem so important.

In the hustle and bustle of life, make sure you take time out!

There can be intemperance in work just as in drink.
C. S. Lewis

Don't overdo things and leave no time for God.

Are you a Mary or a Martha?

'Martha, Martha, . . . you are worried and upset about many things, but only one thing is needed. Mary has chosen what is better, and it will not be taken away from her.'
Luke 10:41, 42

Yes, work is important, but it mustn't crowd out quality time with God. We need to sit at the feet of Jesus to learn of him.

Take a break!

Are you tired? Worn out? . . .
Come to me. Get away with
me and you'll recover your
life. I'll show you how to
take a real rest.
Matthew 11:28, MGE

Jesus offers rest and
restoration.

Feeling tired?

But I have stilled and quieted my soul; like a weaned child with its mother, like a weaned child is my soul within me.
Psalm 131:2

As a child rests in its mother's arms, underneath are your Father's everlasting arms offering *you* peace and rest.

God's remedy for stress

He makes me lie down in green pastures, he leads me beside quiet waters, he restores my soul.
Psalm 23:2, 3

He'll bring you to quiet resting places if you let him lead.

Refocus!

*Drag your thoughts away
from your troubles . . . by
the ears, by the heels, or any
other way you can manage it.*
Mark Twain

Make a determined effort to
concentrate on the positives
in your life.

The power of positive thinking

Finally, brothers, whatever is true, whatever is noble, whatever is right, whatever is pure, whatever is lovely, whatever is admirable – if anything is excellent or praiseworthy – think about such things.
Philippians 4:8

God's prescription for the mind will heal a multitude of ills.

Yes, life's a struggle

Never forget that only dead fish swim with the stream.
Malcolm Muggeridge

But remember that the prize at the end is out of this world!

Ready for battle?

God, who foresaw your tribulation, has specially armed you to go through it, not without pain but without stain.
C. S. Lewis

With God's armour victory is assured.

Down but not out

We are hard pressed on every side, but not crushed; perplexed, but not in despair; persecuted, but not abandoned; struck down, but not destroyed.
2 Corinthians 4:8, 9

You can fight and win all of life's battles because you have a Champion at your side.

Don't know which way to turn?

Your word is a lamp to my feet and a light for my path.
Psalm 119:105

When you need guidance, study God's road map to find out the way.

Enjoy life!

Stop worrying about the potholes in the road and celebrate the journey!
Barbara Hoffman

But make sure you're driving on the narrow and not the broad highway!

Time is valuable

Dost thou love life? Then do not squander time, for that is the stuff life is made of.
Benjamin Franklin

Use yours for God's glory.

Today's the day!

Yesterday is history. Tomorrow is a mystery. And today? Today is a gift. That's why we call it the present.
Babtunde Olatunji

Live for today and let tomorrow worry about itself.

Our high calling

We are called to live in the presence of God, under the authority of God and to the glory of God.
R. C. Sproul

Don't neglect to give your life over to him and spend time with him day by day.

Don't forget to say thank you

This day and your life are God's gift to you: so give thanks and be joyful always!
Jim Beggs

Let your favourite attitude be gratitude.

What's most important?

For where your treasure is,
there your heart will be also.
Matthew 6:21

Is *your* heart in the right
place?

Looking
unto Jesus . . .

If I look at myself, I am depressed.
If I look at those around me, I am
often disappointed.
If I look at my circumstances, I am
discouraged.
But if I look at Jesus, I am constantly,
consistently and eternally filled.
Anon

Where are *you* looking?

Doubt v. Faith

Doubt sees the obstacles
Faith sees the way.
Doubt sees the darkest night
Faith sees the day.
Doubt dreads to take a step
Faith soars on high.
Doubt questions, 'Who believes?'
Faith answers, 'I.'
Anon

Keep your eye focused on
Jesus, the author and finisher
of your faith.

The one to trust

I will say of the Lord, 'He is my refuge and my fortress: my God; in him will I trust.'
Psalm 91:2

God is your Sovereign Protector. Give your life to him and he'll watch over you.

Trust his leading

*Where God guides,
he provides.*
Anon

He will never let you
down.

Believe and receive!

*Faith sees the invisible,
believes the unbelievable,
and receives the impossible.*
Corrie ten Boom

God's power can accomplish
wonderful things in your life.
Just *believe* it!